This is a book about abuse, identity, God's power, and new life. People use those words a lot. Sean's life, creatively retold here, illustrates them in a way few others can. Do you believe in the Holy Spirit and the good news of Jesus Christ? There's no other good explanation for this book. It's a recounting of remarkable and amazing grace.

Jonathan Leeman, Editorial Director, 9Marks

Sean's story is moving and motivating. It is moving to hear him recount how hurt people hurt other people, and it is motivating to hear him recount how God saves sinners. Sean tells his story in a way that makes much of God.

Andy Naselli, Professor of Systematic Theology and New Testament, Bethlehem College and Seminary, Minneapolis, Minnesota

Sean's story is wild. Apart from experiencing God's grace, I don't know how anyone would believe it. And yet, when you taste that grace for yourself, you can't help but agree with Jesus: 'With man this is impossible, but with God all things are possible.' Praise God for his work in and through Sean.

Collin Hansen, Editor-in-Chief, The Gospel Coalition

Wow. What a testimony of God's grace! My heart broke as I read my dear brother's story. It also gave me a fresh appreciation for Romans 5:20: '... where sin increased, grace abounded all the more ....' May the Lord use Rebel to Your Will to help those who may have experienced similar things to feel seen and to see the beauty, power, wisdom and love of our Heavenly Father.

Shai Linne, Recording Artist and Bible Teacher

Sean and I could not have lived more different lives. And yet, God, in his mysterious providence, caused our paths to cross and become fast friends. Reading Sean's story is a powerful reminder that in a world wracked with sin, God is at work making graves into gardens.

Matthew T. Martens, Author, *Reforming Criminal Justice: A Christian Proposal*

Sean DeMars has given us a harrowing insight into his experiences growing up in a family where violence and substance abuse was commonplace and the habits and lifestyle passed through the generations. He writes with brutal honesty by briefly describing episodes of his life which all the more amplify the wonderful grace of God that he becomes a Christian and by God's grace has broken the cycle and is living for Christ and bringing his own children up in the fear and knowledge of the Lord.

Graham Nicholls, Director, Affinity; pastor, Christ Church Haywards Heath, Haywards Heath, UK

Foreword by MARK DEVER

SEAN DEMARS

REBEL

TO

YOUR

WILL

A STORY OF ABUSE, FATHER HUNGER
AND GOSPEL HOPE

Copyright © Sean DeMars 2024

paperback ISBN 978-1-5271-1097-7
ebook ISBN 978-1-5271-1060-1

10 9 8 7 6 5 4 3 2 1

Published in 2024
by
Christian Focus Publications Ltd,
Geanies House, Fearn, Ross-shire,
IV20 1TW, Great Britain.
www.christianfocus.com

Cover design & Typesetting by Francisco Adolfo Hernández Aceves

Printed and bound by
Bell and Bain, Glasgow

CONTENTS

DEDICATION

To my ladybugs:

Three women who,
like Jesus,
love me better than I deserve.

FOREWORD

This is a story of God's grace. Even so, this book is hard to read. But even more, this book is good to read. Sean writes in a staccato style conveying his own experiences of some dark episodes of a broken life. He writes with unvarnished honesty, juxtaposing his experiences as a child with those he and his dear wife Amber are now providing for their own daughters. This makes the book bearable.

The style of the prose along with the stories recounted is brief and vivid. The impressions left are sometimes vague, but suggestive enough to be painfully poignant. Knowing Sean as a Christian, husband, father, friend and pastor I know that he had to be persuaded to share these memories. He is humble enough to let us into his own brokenness, and wise enough not to glorify any of it. There is no attractiveness in the sin Sean recounts.

Why should such a book be written and read? Because it gives us a unique account of God's goodness. "As grace extends to more and more people it may increase thanksgiving, to the glory of God," Paul wrote in 2 Corinthians 4:15. Surely eternity itself will be filled with recounting God's goodness in individual's lives, as more of His holiness and mercy, His creative grace and ingenious kindness, His unfailing justice and His certain providence is revealed. God's manifold wisdom is displayed to the rulers and authorities in the heavenly places through the Church (Eph. 3:10), and that very wisdom is seen in Esther's story. Have you read that story in the Bible?

Esther's story is worth considering here. Esther just happens to be Jewish, and she just happens to be beautiful. Esther just happens to be favored by the king. Mordecai just happens to overhear the plot against the king's life. A report of this just happens to be written in the king's chronicles. Haman just happens to notice someone not kneeling down before him, happens to find out he was a Jew, and then, when he plotted his revenge, the dice just happen to indicate that he should take his revenge almost a year in the future! (What is it Proverbs 16:33 says? "The lot is cast into the lap, but its every decision is from the LORD.")

Then Esther happens to get the king's approval to speak, but then also happens to put off her request for another day. This just happens to send Haman out by Mordecai one more time, which just happens to cause him to recount it to his friends, which just happens to cause them to encourage him to build a scaffold immediately! So Haman just happens to be stirred up to go to the king's presence early the next morning.

And it just so happens that that very same night, the mighty king can't command a moment's sleep, and he just happens to have this book read to him, and in that book, they just happen to read about Mordecai's deed, and they happen to know that Mordecai had not been rewarded. Consider even the fact that Mordecai had just happened not to have been rewarded for saving the king's life! How unusual must that have been?! Could Mordecai even have been resentful at the time of being overlooked? I could go on, but you get the idea.

Nothing in Esther's life, or Sean's—or yours or mine—just happens. At least, not in the sense of happening without God's provident purpose for His own underlying it all. In these pages, Sean recounts everything from being committed to a mental hospital to uncovering soul-sickening corruption and abuse among some false teachers and bad shepherds. All along the way the tragedy of sin is played out in the growing light of confidence in God's overwhelming triumph.

Though I have twice been Sean's pastor and teacher, and am still his friend, I have never had the privilege of being his father. If I were to claim him as any sort of son, I would do so with affection for him, and with amazed thanksgiving to God for what He has done through Sean. I think that you, too, will join me in such thanksgiving after you read this important narrative. This is a story of God's grace.

Mark Dever
Pastor, Capitol Hill Baptist Church

THE BEGINNING

My first memory.

Thirty-some-odd years have passed since that terrible night. I'm there again, in the reddish hue of the room. A tequila sunset breaks through the smoke-darkened curtains. The air is acrid, heavy with sweat and stale vomit. Virginia Slim cigarette smoke curls up from the ashtray on the nightstand. The smell of Jim Beam fogs out from her breath, rolling hard over my nose and mouth. I feel her lips on my neck. She calls me by a name I don't know, the name of a man I've never met. Her tongue slips out and moves along my face. My young heart fills with fear and confusion. Panic. I bolt out of the bed, yelling behind me that I just need to use the bathroom and "I'll be right back."

But I don't come back. I lock myself in the bathroom and sit quickly on the wooden toilet seat. I cry, but I don't want to. I need to be quiet. I hope she doesn't hear me. Maybe she'll fall sleep. I listen for the sound of footsteps but hear none.

I can still feel the texture of that bathroom door, the wood thin and splintered as my fingers glide sideways across it. I can still hear the muffled sound of her voice calling out to me somewhere from the middle distance of our tiny home. Calling me back into that room. Calling me back to bed. She cries out for me in anger. And then sadness. And then not at all. Silence.

My chubby little hands fold into a pretzel. I pray. I weep quietly. I ask God to help me, to protect me. That prayer was my first, most desperate, most sincere communication with God. I was six years old. Did he hear me? I slept on the cold floor until morning.

Why am I writing this book? It's hard to say. Why are you reading it? Consider the great and powerful autobiographies of Christian history: Elizabeth Elliot, George Mueller, Augustine of Hippo, etc. And then there's me—Sean DeMars. "Who is Sean DeMars?" No one. Nothing. Consider…

> For if anyone thinks he is something, when he is nothing, he deceives himself.
>
> Gal. 6:3

And yet, there may be a story here worth telling.

> From now on, therefore, we regard no one according to the flesh. Even though we once regarded Christ according to the flesh, we regard him thus no longer. Therefore, if anyone is in Christ, he is a new creation. The old has passed away; behold, the new has come. All this is from God, who through Christ reconciled us to himself and gave us the ministry of reconciliation.
>
> 2 Cor. 5:16-18

Other Christians have been telling me to tell and retell my story for as long as I've been saved. And so I will.

My daughters glide through the air, giggling on the swing hanging from an oak branch in our front yard. Patience is eight, Isabella is six, and I love them more than all love clichés combined. I watch them through the kitchen window. The world is a dark and scary place, but they are babes in evil. They dance in the driveway and build a fort in the backyard. They fear nothing other than chores and homework. Breathe in the Americana.

THE FENCE

The chain link fence around my childhood home was a mile high (or so it seemed), with sharp prongs jutting violently from the top, two by two, all the way around my prison grounds. Rusted diamond links formed the chain wall protecting the tiny house on Albemarle Street. I once saw a man try to come through the fence, body full of stab wounds, blood staining the cement like an oil leak.

Behind the house was a small thin strip of brown grass, a shed, and a clothesline that I loved to hang from as a boy. The poles were more rust than metal, their arms akimbo in the sun, clothes held in place by wooden pins from the bucket by the shed. The living room carpet was a deep green shag, covered in cigarette ash and cat urine. We spent many nights in the bathtub, ostensibly to keep us safe from stray bullets.

THE TV TRAY

The Kirkham family has been kind enough to invite me over for a meal and a game of UNO. They love me well. We laugh and joke and laugh again. I'm having the best night of my life. I've never felt so normal. In an attempt to really blow the roof off with laughter, I stop eating, fold to the right, and pass gas. Loudly. The table grows silent, the younger children snicker, the mother kindly pretends as if nothing has happened, and the patriarch leans in and puts his warm, heavy hand on my shoulder.

"We don't pass gas at the table. It's kind of rude. No big deal." A smile and a wink. He slaps me on the back and the meal moves on. I smile, blink away my tears, and take a big bite of food. I'm mortified. I've offended these people who, secretly, I want to be my family.

I'm eighteen years old, and this is my first family dinner. I feel like I'm in a movie.

"Pass the green beans."

"Can you hand me the mashed potatoes, please?"

"No hitting! And make sure you say please and thank you."

So Hollywood didn't make this stuff up; this is what real families do.

Most of my childhood meals were eaten on a metal TV tray, in my bedroom, in front of the television. The antenna was crude, always in need of adjustment, helped greatly by two balls of aluminum foil tipping the end of each rabbit ear. We changed the channel with a pair of pliers and slapped the side of the box whenever the picture grew fuzzy.

My TV tray had golden legs and a dark wood-patterned plastic cover curling in at each corner. It was heavy, squeaky and always at the foot of my bed. When my mother was sober, she would serve my favorite food in my room. TV on, tray open, door closed, sins atoned for.

THE SUMMER OF
HOT DOGS

I can eat hot dogs now. Barely. For the longest time, I couldn't stomach the sight of a frankfurter. Somewhere around the age of nine or ten (or eight, for all I know—the years all run together now) my mother stayed drunk or high (or both) for the entire summer. She rarely came to consciousness long enough to prepare any meals, so food was up to me. Our small freezer was packed full of beef hotdogs as if she had planned her summer-long, drug-induced hibernation.

I would thaw a pack of frozen wieners every other day or so. I ate two hot dogs for every meal of every day—breakfast, lunch and dinner. Two hotdogs, always prepared the same way—microwaved in an empty Country Crocket butter bowl. (The poor man's Tupperware.) Here's the recipe (and please don't share; it's a family secret.) Fill the bowl halfway up with water, toss in the dogs, microwave for forty-five seconds, shake the dogs dry, lay each on a piece of bread. Ketchup, mustard, and relish if we had it. Take a bite, chew, scrape the soggy bread from the roof of your mouth. Repeat. All. Summer. Long.

The next summer was better on the food front. My

mother's addiction was worse than ever, but I had learned how to steal money from her purse when there was money to steal. The habit was this: wait until I was sure she was comatose, grab money from the purse, walk down to the taqueria, and buy tacos and mountain dew. Eat tacos. Tacos are still my favorite food.

Amber places her left hand on my right forearm as we drive. It never gets old. I melt every time. I reach up and grab her firmly by the back of the neck. I squeeze and dig into the knots on her shoulders. "Hey, it's not fair that mom gets lovins and we don't!" I contort my shoulders and reach back to squeeze the knees of my little ladybugs. I love to love them. I love scratching, squeezing, pinching, hugging, kissing, tickling, and blowing raspberries. Because I love them, I also discipline them. The rod of correction drives foolishness far from the heart of children. But they know that I will never discipline them in anger. They know that even the hand of discipline is an expression of tender, fatherly love.

FEAR

Most of my young life was lived in fear. Walking through a doorway past my mother was always a risk. Would she hit me as I passed? The odds were 70/30 against me. Car rides were always a time of great anxiety. I would press myself into the driver's side door, shoulders slanted down and away, head on a swivel, ready to turn my cheek into the window and hide my face from her back hand. The gold ring on her right ring finger could catch me like a knife's edge.

She was creative with her beatings. She would use anything to hurt me. She once used a long, thin plastic curtain rod, each lash like a fire whip. Car antenna, belt (the buckled end), frying pan, extension cord, TV tray (you remember the TV tray from earlier?): if she could swing it or throw it, she would use it. These were the objects that she'd use for the lengthier sessions, but there were also the random kicks, punches, slaps, hair pulls, and glass ashtrays to the head.

Some days lasted longer than the allotted twenty-four hours. She would fly into a rage, back me into a corner, rain down blows on me until she could no longer move her arms. She would send me to my room until she was ready to start again. The door would open, she would swing the belt and time would come to a complete stop.

I can't remember it all now. I only see in snapshots. Impressions, really. I remember the scent of her perfume, the fade of her tattoos, and the smell of whiskey on her breath. I can hear the sound of her crying on the kitchen floor. I can see her tearing out her hair in the car, screaming at me, wanting to know where we would go next. I can feel her weight sag over me as I drag her home again. She's fine, thanks for asking. She's just really tired.

We've been sitting in the car for several hours. It's hot. Southern California summer hot. The ruby red sky is folding into the horizon. A silver-haired citizen knocks on the passenger's side window. We've parked in her yard, apparently, the back half of the vehicle hanging diagonally off the curb. She sees an eight-year-old boy sweating in his seat and a woman asleep behind the wheel. She asks if I'm OK. I nod that I am as I behold the stranger in her nightgown. She moves around the front of the car to the other side and raps gently on the glass. My mother doesn't move. The woman taps again. Still nothing. I reach over and shake my mother until her eyes open unevenly, uncomprehendingly. The kind citizen is greeted with a barrage of swears and insults as my mother turns from me to the woman still gently tapping on the driver's side window. The woman backs away, fearful and walks inside. My mother starts the car, cracks me with the back of her fist, and drives away, sideswiping several vehicles along the way, swearing at each offender in passing. She's drunk. She's been drunk for a week. We make it home in one piece. She crawls into bed and sleeps for many moons.

There is a kind of joy in the anticipation of a good thing, but there is also a deep dread in the anticipation of a terrible thing. Sometimes my mother's rage was instantaneous: a back hand, a hair pull, a kick, a car door slamming on my husky little leg. Other times, however, she would signal her wrath from a distance, walking towards me with jaw clenched, lips curled over her teeth, fire in her eyes.

I sit in the car, waiting, fearing, trying not to cry. She hates it when I cry, mocking me relentlessly. I have a direct line of sight on her as she emerges from the parent-teacher conference. She laughs, smiles and chats graciously with my teacher before turning towards me in the car. I see her see me and begin to cry. I see her face dim, from light to dark, and I know what's coming.

She is rarely silent as she beats me. I was a mistake. I should have never been born. *Punch.* She hates me. I'm a disgusting fat pig. *Back hand.* F word this, F word that, she should have had an abortion. *Hair pull.* Long hair pull, yanking my chubby little cheeks this way and that for minutes on end. This usually lasted all the way home. Traffic was the worst. She was free to focus on the task at hand.

The routine is always the same: she beats me all the way down the freeway, through the neighborhood and up the driveway. I rush out of the car, rush into the house and under the covers. The screen door swings open and then slams shut behind her. My bedroom door crashes wide open. The covers fly from my body, revealing me curled up in the fetal position on my ninja turtle bedsheets. And then her belt turns the room white with pain.

Sometimes the beatings are pure. Blow after blow. No talking. No screaming. Just grunting and groaning and the heavy breathing of a pack–a–day smoker. Sometimes she cries. With heavy sobs, she tells me she's sorry. Sometimes she apologizes, even as she beats me. Still other times, she likes to whistle while she works. She talks to me, telling me she should have had an abortion. She warns me that the Mexicans next door are going to eat me if I don't watch out and start behaving. She tells me about myself. I'm a fat, ugly piece of *#!*. Nobody loves me. Nobody will ever love me. She doesn't love me.

I walk my daughters to school. Amber is on the right, I'm on the left. The ladybugs sit between us. We review our catechism questions, kick pinecones and make sure not to step on any cracks in the sidewalk (to protect Mom's back, of course). We stop at the entrance of the school where we sit down on the bench and pray. Dear Jesus, help my girls to do all things to the glory of Your name, to honor their teachers, and to be kind to those who need a friend. Amen.

SCHOOL

I attended a small Seventh-Day Adventist school in my early years, paid for by my well-to-do grandmother. I learned to read, write and kind of do arithmetic. The teachers were fine, I suppose, if not painfully naïve.

It wasn't uncommon for me to stay out of school long enough to let my bruises heal. On one occasion, a beating had left me with two black eyes, one side worse than the other. When she sobered up, she saw my face and cried. She told me she was sorry and that it would never happen again. She said this almost every time, and I think she really believed it. She made it up to me by making my favorite dinner—tacos. I ate five. Tacos are still my favorite food.

THE CRY FOR HELP

My first day back in school I raise my hand and ask to use the restroom. I take a black marker with me, which I use to color in the dark spot under my right eye. I want the black eye to look fresh and dark like it had been a few days prior. I walk back into the classroom circumspect, hide the marker, and take my place on the alphabet carpet. I am in equal parts afraid and desperate to be seen. A short time later, Ms. Kathy, my teacher, sees my eye and scolds me for coloring on my face. Why would I do such a thing? Go to the bathroom and wash that off right away.

Nobody ever asked me if everything was OK at home. Not when I colored my own eye black, not when I would flinch fearfully in her presence, not when I would hide during pick up time at school. Never. Not a teacher, not a family member, not a friend; nobody ever asked if I was OK. Looking back now, I wonder if the ignorance was legitimate or willful. Maybe it was both.

A few years later, at a different school, I sit silently in class and work on my assignment. As I work, I hear her voice faintly on the wind. She's calling out to me, screaming at the top of her lungs in a drunken stupor. The sound of her voice moves closer and closer to the classroom, and then further and further away. I wait at my desk, terrified, embarrassed, anxious. The principal calls me out of class and into the office. There she stands, drunk, cigarette in hand, braless in her nightgown, telling me it's time to go.

Nobody stopped her. Nobody protected me. We drove away. Swerve, swerve, swerve, all the way home.

HER STORY

My mother had a hard life. The daughter of a drug addict mother, she was abused mercilessly, abandoned, demeaned and neglected. She knew a man for the first time at the age of eleven and was raped shortly thereafter. She was molested by a family member and introduced to drugs at a very young age. She was a compulsive liar, but I'm inclined to believe her stories of wire hanger beatings and other forms of childhood torture.

Hurt people hurt people. She hurt me out of a place of deep and abiding pain. And she hurt me bad. Towards the end of her life, as she lay dying with cancer, I tried to pity her. I tried to consider the shape of her life and the depth of her suffering. I wish I could say it was easy. I wish I could say that I found grace flowing out of my heart like a mighty river. In reality, grace was like the drip, drip, drip of a leaky faucet. I found grace at odd intervals and never enough to fill the cup of my heart. Or hers. I've forgiven her, by God's grace, as I have been forgiven. But still I look back on those dying days, wishing I could have loved her better.

We open the door of the hotel room and my ladybugs blow past me to claim their space. They jump on the bed, swim in the overly-chlorinated pool, and eat yummy pancakes at the continental breakfast dining room. They love going to hotels, and I love that they love it. They'll never clean up my vomit or beg me to wake up for fear that I've overdosed. Their memories of sleeping in the family car will be happy ones, long naps on fun road trips with sing-alongs and games and gas station pit stops for snacks. Last one to the car is a rotten egg!

THE DEEP SOUTH

I was born in Northridge, California, but lived much of my childhood in San Diego: Chula Vista, National City, Paradise Hills, Bonita and Imperial Beach. Momma was a rolling stone. Eviction notices as far as the eye can see. From house to apartment, apartment to hotel, hotel to car. You can't really get evicted from your car, unless your car gets towed. Ours never did.

The hotels are fun at first, but the descent into misery is steep: From Ramada to Motel 6 to a room with hissing cockroaches and blood-stained linen. There is no school during this time, just a lot of sitting around waiting for my mother to come in off the streets with money for food. I never know how much money she makes, but I know it's enough for cigarettes, booze, drugs, and a few days' food.

We acquire a single eye stove, a pan and a cooler that we fill with free ice from the motel ice machine. She makes enough hamburger helper (minus the hamburger) to last two or three days. When the booze runs out, the cigarettes run low, or the food goes bad, she goes out to make her money again. I must not open the door for anyone. I must not leave the room. Just watch TV until she gets back. From Looney Tunes to Nick at Night, from Melrose Place to Hogan's Heroes and Happy Days. I sit at the edge of the hotel bed and fill my eyes with the light of Hollywood.

The motel days are scary and boring, but better than the car. The car we often call home is a hatchback two door Geo Storm. I won it on my birthday at Disneyland. I pulled the lever and a car came up out of the ground. I was told I could choose the color. I wanted canary yellow but ended up with a dark blue. Such is life.

When we sleep in the car she curls up in the back seat and I lean the passenger side chair back and turn into the door with my baby blue blanket and Randy, my favorite stuffed animal. I'm too old for a stuffed animal, but can't sleep without him. Sleeping in the car is tricky and not just because of bodily logistics. Where can we park for the night without being harassed? What do we do during the day when there's nowhere to go, no money for gas, and nothing to do but sit? How does one live without a bathroom, kitchen or bedroom?

She would occasionally find a man for us to stay with, most of whom were kind enough. But it never lasted. She would set herself on fire with insanity and we would be back on the street before hope had time to sink in. Sometimes, the men who sent us packing pitied us enough to shell out a few bucks for another motel room. Good enough.

I walk through the door and call the family together in the kitchen. I place the treat on the table in the nook and grab a kitchen knife from my wife's avant-garde butcher's block. We gather around the table and read the package together: maple bacon peppermint chocolate bar. I tear open the wrapping with a husky eagerness, carefully measure the bar, and then cut it into thirds. I give the three pieces to the three women around the table. Bella doesn't like it. Of course. Patience loves it and wants Bella's piece if she's not going to eat it. Of course. Amber loves it just because it's chocolate. Of course.

THE VENDING MACHINE

I watch my mother put four quarters into the vending machine and move her index finger towards the keypad. I don't ask, but I hope she's going to finally buy me the Crunch bar I've been eyeing for weeks now. I've been obsessing over it, literally dreaming about it. My only comfort in life is food. My only joy is in the taste of something sweet. Her broken red nail presses a letter key and then a number key. A brown box the size of a deck of playing cards falls from the silver coil and lands lightly in the tray below. What's in the box, mom?

Nothing.

She puts me in the bathroom with a Gameboy and tells me not to come out until she calls for me. I hear the door open, then a man's muffled voice, and then I get lost in Zelda until she calls me back into the room. I watch TV, eat dinner, and crawl under the covers for bed.

Later, while she's sleeping, I steal quarters from her wallet and go to the vending machine. Ignoring the clerk behind the desk, I press the buttons that correspond to the cardboard box. The coil moves, the box falls, and I steal away with my prize. I stand beneath the metal stairs outside the room and tear the cardboard top away. I drop the prize into my hand. It's light and round and red. It's a condom. I'm very, very disappointed that I didn't get that Crunch bar. Looking back on those days I am thankful that in her darkest hour, she had the wherewithal, at least sometimes, to use protection.

Frequently, I am in the same small room with her as she takes men to bed. I lay on the floor and hear her carry out the sex act in the bed above. The routine is just that, a routine: The man asks if she's sure I'm really asleep… if she's sure I'm not awake. She assures him that I'm asleep and that everything is fine. He climbs into bed. Movement, noise, breathing, grunting, silence. She locks the door behind the man as he passes back into the night. I am practiced at lying motionless, pretending to sleep until she gets out of the shower, at which point she "wakes me up" and gives me my rightful place in the bed next to her. I hide myself as close to the edge as possible, shuddering whenever her skin touches mine.

It all comes to an end one night in a seedy motel parking lot somewhere in the San Diego area. I sit on the edge of the bed, glued to the TV, waiting for her to knock so I can pull the chain and open the door, like always. Suddenly, the door begins to thunder. She screams and cries and heaves her way into the room as I pull the door cautiously open. She crashes to the floor and stays there sobbing for a long time. She's been raped.

WHAT'S IN ALABAMA?

We moved to Alabama shortly after the night of her sorrow. Her plan was to get clean and we were going to move across the country to make it happen. She'd tried to get clean before, but the sobriety never lasted. I spent many childhood nights in smoke-filled rooms listening to people introduce themselves as addicts. But the meetings never worked, and her sobriety never lasted. This time was different. She really did get clean in Alabama.

Mostly.

She used mild doses of Xanax and oxycodone to keep herself away from the booze, coke, etc. I was very young through most of her addiction struggles, so I don't know exactly what her drug of choice was, but I do know that if there was a drug around, she would do it. One day, I walked into our living room to find her naked, starfished on the couch, furiously breathing into a rag held over her nose and mouth. I learned later, in my teenage years, that she was huffing paint. Later I preferred to huff duster, but to each his own, I guess.

*I live less than two miles from a Chick-Fil-A.
Life is good. Our four-bedroom home has
a detached garage where I work out with
several members of our local church. My wife
has turned one of the bedrooms into an art
studio where she makes custom t-shirts and
refurbishes furniture. Our closets are full, our
fridge is fully stocked, and the temperature
of our home is controlled down to the very
degree. 72 degrees is too hot, but 71 is
just right.*

*My wife sings 'Jesus Loves Me', This I know
as she lays our girls down to bed every night.
Bells tells me no tickling tonight, and I agree.
And then I tickle her until she can't breathe.
I love my little ladybugs; I'll see you in the
morning. I turn off the light, close the door,
and sit down on my very comfortable couch.
Each child finds a reason to get out of bed at
least twice. We are frustrated in the moment,
but will miss the bedtime dance in the days
to come.*

MADE FOR TV MOVIE

Upon arrival in Alabama we move into a brick house in a quaint neighborhood. It's the kind of place where little girls can sell lemonade and industrious young men can mow lawns for money in the summer. We move in with my grandmother and great-grandmother; three women and me. My great-grandmother, the matriarch of the family, is in the throes of deep dementia. She was once a very lovely lady thrice married, a hair stylist to the stars, and quite wealthy. When her last husband died, her mind went with him. My mother spent the next year forging checks in her name, siphoning tens of thousands of dollars from her retirement account.

If there were ever three women who couldn't live under the same roof together, it was my mother, grandmother and great-grandmother. A generational curse. They fought constantly, each hateful samurai slicing and slashing their verbal katanas swiftly in battle. I don't mind, really, because my mother spends so much time in battle with my grandmother that the beatings slow down considerably.

Much could be said of our transition from southern California to north Alabama, but perhaps we should stick to the high points. There were no black people hanging from trees (as I had been told there would be), very few tractors, and not a single pair of overalls in sight. What I found, instead, was a community of ordinary people, kind, generous, sinful and annoyingly religious. Even the gangsters loved their grandmas and went to church on Sunday.

Things began to go south (no pun intended) when we moved out of my grandmother's house. My mother worked at a grocery store first, then as a waitress at the Waffle House. We lived on welfare, replete with state-sponsored insurance, Section 8 housing, and food stamps. The beatings increased, but never returned to the severity or duration of my younger years. She would still scream and cuss and say things that no one should ever say to another human, much less a mother to her only begotten son.

She grew increasingly neurotic in those days. On the one hand, she became a neat freak. She would fly off the handle if the magazines on the coffee table were not arranged just so. On the other hand, our two-bedroom apartment was drenched with cat urine, teaming with fleas, and filled floor to ceiling with stale cigarette smoke. (After her eviction, they had to replace the carpet down to the sub-flooring.)

I began to have the first semblance of a normal childhood at this time. We didn't live in the best neighborhood, but I was finally able to play outside with boys my age. I would swim in the summer, play football in the fall, and struggle with school all year long. I never managed to make up all that lost time away from the classroom. I also never really tried very hard to do so.

The day she stopped beating me was the day I realized

I could stop her.

I'm playing outside with some friends when she calls me from the front door of our apartment. I respond with typical thirteen-year-old lip. You couldn't write better back-talk if you tried. She lets fly the dogs of war, demanding (to my embarrassment) that I get my ass upstairs immediately before she kicks it in front of all my little friends. I rush towards the stairs and meet her in her fury halfway up the flight. She hits me in the face as hard as she can. I absorb the blow without flinching and set my face like flint. She sees, and I see that she sees, that we are done; she will never hit me again.

I wish I could say that that was the last time she hurt me, but it wasn't. She merely shifted tactics. From then on out, her sole aim was to ravage me with her words. And she did. Hurt people hurt people. Though my body had grown big and strong and resilient to her fists, my heart and mind were still weak within me, vulnerable to her words.

I'm a grinch.

But my wife finally convinces me to get a Christmas tree. I agree, on the condition that it's fake. I refuse to spend money on a Christmas tree every year. I will not deal with the hassle of putting it up, taking it down, and hauling it out to the alley. You can only ask so much of a man.

It's Thanksgiving Day.

The tree is up, pajamas are on, and we're ready to decorate. But one thing is missing. If we're going to do this, we might as well do it right. I pull up the classic Christmas music playlist on iTunes and scroll, looking for just the right song. I know it as soon as I see it. 'Jingle Bell Rock' by Bobby Helms.

We have special ornaments to hang first, ornaments that best represent each member of the family. Amber got a pink converse, I got a taco, Patience got a donut, and Bella got a unicorn. We decorate the tree for a few minutes until I have to step into the kitchen. I'm crying uncontrollably. My grinch heart is growing three sizes, and it hurts. I look at my girls smiling as they glide around the tree with tinsel, ornaments and glee. Their faces glow like gold. Merry Christmas, everyone.

MERRY CHRISTMAS

I'm fourteen years old. It's Christmas Eve. I'm threatening suicide again and she is encouraging me to be a man of action. I accept her offer in spite and run to the medicine cabinet where I swallow as many pills as I can find. She watches me swallow each handful with a look of mild amusement. Merry Christmas, everyone.

I'm strapped to the gurney at the wrists and feet. A silver dollar-sized plastic donut is inserted between my teeth to keep my mouth open as the tube is inserted down into my stomach. As soon as the tube touches the back of my throat I begin to vomit. I try to breathe through my nose, but can't. I begin to panic. Within seconds the tube is all the way in and the nurse suctions the vomit from around my nose and mouth. A clear, cold liquid flows out of a large syringe and through the tube. Moments later, another large syringe pulls the same fluid up out of my stomach and into a medical grade trash bag. I watch, from outside of myself, as the half-digested pills dance in the liquid flowing up through the tube and into the bag.

You know your stomach is done being pumped when you begin to see more bile than clear liquid flow through the tube. Then they administer the liquid charcoal to catch anything that the pumping may have missed. Then they pull the tube out, wipe you down, clean you up, and give you a little valium to help you sleep.

SO IT BEGINS...

I, the LORD your God, am a jealous God, visiting
the iniquity of the fathers on the children, and on
the third and the fourth generations of those who
hate Me.

Deut 5:9-10

Fathers shall not be put to death for their sons, nor
shall sons be put to death for their fathers; everyone
shall be put to death for his own sin.

Deut 24:16

I smoke my first cigarette at the age of twelve. It's not
particularly enjoyable, but it's cool. I want to be cool, so I
keep at it, mastering the art and science of it all. Learning
how to hold the cigarette just right, ashing with ease, and
rolling the cigarette around my mouth like a pro. Soon
enough I am offered weed, which I smoke for the first time
to no effect. I try again shortly thereafter, this time in the
woods behind my apartment complex. A neighbor boy
and I smoke a poorly rolled joint and spend the rest of the
afternoon looking up at the ceiling as electricity dances
across our field of vision.

I always told myself I would never be like my mother.

(Yes, that old trope.) I told myself that I hated her, I would never be like her, I would never do drugs. Yet here I am, not only doing drugs, but soon enough stealing and selling drugs in order to pay for my habit. Soon enough I can be found walking around with a pistol in my pants and a real attitude problem. This is, of course, to make a long story short.

Like my childhood hero, Tupac, I was not a natural born gangster. I was instinctively tender-hearted, gentle towards the weak, and very fearful. I loved art and was bent towards all things creative. But I learned to be hard. My first fight was in the community pool on a warm summer evening.

The sky is orange, the water is blue, and a splash fight turns into a fist fight in the soft shade of the shallow end. I break my right pinky knuckle in the melee and the skin on my middle knuckle flaps back into a V-shape from a blow to his front tooth. I walk away from that contest feeling, for the first time, the thrill of violence. I taste blood and I like it. I begin to fight every chance I get, and if a chance doesn't arise, I create one out of thin air. Hurt people hurt people.

I was institutionalized for the first time at the age of fourteen: a mental hospital. My first roommate had Tourette syndrome and would wake me up at all hours of the night with spitting and cussing and crying. I was placed in the psych ward many times throughout the years. My final stay was in the adult ward with a man who, on more than one occasion, rubbed his fecal matter on the floor, ceiling and walls of our shared bathroom. I tried repeatedly to escape, but only managed to clear the entrance once.

I see a counselor carrying a stack of Styrofoam to-go plates precariously towards the exit door of the dining room. It is a sturdy, metal door. The lock is magnetized and can only be opened with an access card. The counselor fumbles for her card with one hand as she balances the tray full of food with the other. I rush to the aid of the damsel in distress. I hold the trays for her as she unlocks and opens the door. She thanks me for being such a helpful young man. I hand her the food and immediately bolt towards the front door of the hospital. She screams behind me, calling for them to lockdown the exits. It's too late. I fly through the front door and race out of the parking lot, nothing but knees and elbows.

I'm a heavy smoker. Two packs of Newport shorts a day, plus weed, plus huffing air duster, plus crystal meth. I run as fast as I can, which is very slow indeed. The first footsteps I hear behind me belong to a Nigerian worker on the ward. He's a soccer player. He's fast, but small. He grabs me, but I shake him off. I turn around, take off my shirt, and square up for a fight. He backs away. The next person to show up is built like a football player. He's slow, but strong. I swing at him first and miss. I can barely breathe. The fight lasts all of twenty seconds. I'm tackled, hog tied, and carried back into the facility, nothing but knees and elbows.

I graduated from psychiatric care to incarceration at the age of fifteen. I was placed in a wilderness facility in Paint Rock Valley, Alabama. Think: prison, but on the side of a mountain. We cooked food over campfires, went to the bathroom in the ground, chopped wood, shoveled horse manure, and held group therapy sessions by the firelight. I managed to escape this facility as well, but only once, and paid dearly for doing so.

CUTTER

It is a beautiful morning in Paint Rock Valley. The autumn air is crisp and clean, but not cold. A low fog hangs in the valley basin as I tap the side of my head against the cool brick wall. No pain. Thin red lines zig zag the outside of my arms and shoulders. The white meat of my forearms is crosshatched with the wounds of my frustration. I've been cutting myself. Why? It's hard to say. I've heard it said that you cut so that the physical pain overwhelms the emotional pain of trauma. That sounds almost right. But there's more to the story, for sure (Mark 5:1-13)

I turn to face the valley as I gently knock the back of my head against the brick. Pain, but not much. Another crack of the skull, but this time for real. It hurts, but not as bad as I thought it would. Finally, with a deep breath, I bow my head down to my waist and heave it back against the wall. The earth moves quickly towards my face. The sensation of the rough exterior of the brick is gone, replaced by the gritty, gravelly sensation of concrete on the left side of my face. The ground is cold and coarse against my cheek. I want to lift my head, but can't. A forearm grinds my chin and cheekbone into the ground. I've been here before. It's a restraint. Two counselors hold me down to protect me from myself and others. This is my third restraint of the day, and it's only 9 a.m.

I start a fight with a fellow inmate in the shower. The other inmates swarm me. I lay in the shower crying for a long time. The days grow darker. More restraints. More beatings. More cutting. I run towards the edge of a cliff with the hopes of hurling myself off it, only to be tackled from the rear a few feet shy of the edge. I rage constantly. I cry constantly. I am tortured by staff and inmates alike. I stop bathing. They force me to bathe. They come for me in the night or out by the privy. I begin to urinate and defecate on myself for protection.

Twenty years later, I'm chatting casually in the car with two members of my local church when I notice how close we are to Paint Rock Valley, the place where I lost a year of my life. I ask them if they mind a little detour. They oblige. We eventually find the road that leads to the wilderness facility I once called home. The sign posted at the entrance forbids trespassers. That's us. I try to tell them what my life was like in this place. The violence. The torture. The fear. They nod as they listen, attentive and empathetic. But they don't understand. How could they?

Abuse is lonely. You feel alone in the moment, and then you feel alone for the rest of your life as you try and tell your story, if you try and tell it at all. You want those who love you to know you. All of you. But the world you inhabit is a world they cannot know. They can't enter into that suffering with you. They can watch you suffer. They can hurt for you as you hurt. But they can't know what you know, or feel what you feel, for better or worse. I try and end on a lighter note by telling them a funny story, and then we load up and drive away.

After a year in the wild, I'm released back into civilization. Upon reentry I'm placed in alternative school, assigned to outpatient counseling, and come under the care of a social worker. Within months I'm back to selling drugs, failing every class that requires even a modicum of effort, and expelled for violently assaulting a fellow student.

My next hope is Job Corps, a ministry of the US Department of Labor, wherein at-risk youth may receive an assortment of vocational training. I am sent to Bowling Green, Kentucky, with the aim of being trained to be a medical care specialist. I spend most of my time chasing women and drugs. In a few months' time, I am involved in a massive, riot-like affair that leads to my expulsion. I ride a Greyhound bus back to Alabama with twenty-five dollars in my pocket, which I lose at a bus stop in Tennessee trying to buy drugs. Long story short, I got robbed at knife point.

I was placed in many more institutions along the way. Bootcamps, halfway houses, rehab facilities, you name it. Nothing worked. I grew more angry, violent, and addicted with each passing day. At the age of seventeen, I started using crystal meth. Here's how it came to pass.

I used to break into cars at night, stealing car stereos (among other things) to trade for drugs. One day I was put into contact with a handsome young Mexican gentleman who wanted to buy my stolen goods. He was out of weed, he told me, but had something even better. He held out a sandwich bag full of clear crystal shards. I thought it was crack at first, even though crack is more yellow than clear, more chunky than glassy. He told me it was meth and said I could have some for free if I thought I could sell it. I told him that I couldn't because my business was in

REBEL TO YOUR WILL

the projects, not the trailer park. He told me to give it a try anyways, and I did. I took my first hit of meth an hour later, and I knew after I exhaled the first drag that I would kill someone for a second hit. I had done many drugs before this, but nothing moved me quite like methamphetamines.

I sat in the corner of a dark room pointing my pistol at the door, ready to shoot the first person who walks through it. I haven't slept for days. I'm convinced I'm going to be assassinated by the Mexican Mafia. This is not an unreasonable assumption. I've been hiding for a while, for how long I cannot say; the days begin to run together. I've seen what the Mexican Mafia can do to those who cross them and am terrified of what they will do to me for stealing from them. So I sit, for what seems like an eternity, in the corner of the room, staring unflinchingly at the door, hoping no one will walk through it.

I'm seventeen, living in a ratty two-bedroom apartment with my partner in crime. Our business is two-pronged: we sold drugs and pimped teenage girls. This was perhaps the darkest period of my life, which is really saying something, all things considered. I had experienced much sadness prior to this time, but most of the pain was inflicted upon me by others. During this era, I was the inflictor. I won't give you the gruesome details. Just remember what I told you earlier: hurt people hurt people.

BLINDED BY THE LIGHT

There are many ways to smoke meth, but only one surefire way to blind yourself while getting high: Free base on aluminum foil (shiny side up). It's simple, really; you fold a square of tin foil in half, sprinkle some meth along the crease, and place the lighter flame underneath. The meth melts and the vapor rises. It's all about balance. Too far away from the foil and the flame won't melt the meth. Too close to the foil and the meth gets too hot, too fast, and begins to pop like bacon grease. The higher you get, the harder it is to balance.

I sit on the ratty couch, straw in-between my teeth, foil in one hand, lighter in the other, slowly inhaling my own death, when I lose my balance. The hot bacon grease pop is a bullseye, landing in the center of my right eye and blinding me immediately. My vision slowly returns over the next two weeks, but the interim recovery period is a time of great distress. It's not easy to smoke meth with one eye, but I manage.

I hit the back left corner of a black SUV going seventy in a thirty. I'm driving like my life depends on it...because it does. I haven't slept in days. There's a 9mm in my lap and about twenty grand worth of ice under my seat.

The guys chasing me are shoot first, ask questions later kind of guys. I see the SUV flip in my rear view. I can't stop because they're still chasing me. I call one of my side-pieces and tell her to open her garage door and be ready to close it quickly behind me when I pull in. I slam into the back wall of the garage and fly into the quaint suburban home, wild-eyed and gun drawn. I hold her and her two younger siblings hostage for the next hour while I stare out the window in unflinching paranoia.

All is quiet. The hour is late. The lights are off and the garage is empty. I lift my right leg and throw it powerfully at the front door. The frame splinters near the knob as the door flies violently into the dark hallway. I make my way to the gun safe in the back bedroom. I pick the lock, just like she showed me. In less than a minute I pull out of the driveway with a trunk full of guns. My single, solitary pistol doesn't feel like it's offering me the kind of protection I need against the kind of people who are chasing me.

I should feel better…safer. But I don't. I'm afraid to go back to the trap house where they may be looking for me, so I cruise the midnight hours snorting meth out of a Vick's inhaler, triple checking my rearview mirror for anyone who may be following.

I wake up to a police officer tapping the driver side window with his Maglite. The engine is running and my brights are on. He searches the car, finds the guns, and places me under arrest. I'm eighteen years old, which means that I am finally fit to undergo the right of passage I had long expected: I'm finally going to prison.

My little ladybugs love going to church.
They wake up on Sunday morning excited to
spend the morning with the body of Christ.
They color quietly in the pew during the
(very long) sermon. They play hide and seek
in the dusty, old, squirrel-infested building
with their friends. They eat potato salad at
the church potluck and learn the story of the
gospel in Sunday School. This is the only life
they have ever known. They love their daddy.
They love big hugs and back scratches
and dessert night. They may not love their
spankings, but one day they will see the
rod as an instrument of love (Prov. 22:15).
This is the only Sean they know. They will
never meet the drug-dealing, gang-banging,
womanizing, burglarizing, cheating, thieving
blasphemer I once was. Hurt people hurt
people. But those who have been called by
grace become new creations.

AMAZING GRACE

Shortly after my arrest, I was accepted into a program that offered a last chance to young adult offenders. The agreement with the judge was simple: if I graduated the program, I wouldn't have to do time. I was relieved to have the chance to avoid the penitentiary, and so I entered into the facility willing to do whatever was asked of me; even go to church. The program was simple. Do your chores, attend your meetings, pass your drug tests, and go to work and church. The facility was like many others I had attended, but with one major difference: it was faith-based. Jesus, Jesus, Jesus. Jesus all the time.

I wasn't a fan.

I had my first experience with Christianity as a teenager. I was invited by a neighbor boy to something called a youth group, which—to the uninitiated—can be a very strange experience. At the age of thirteen, on a Wednesday night, I walked into a dimly lit garage full of pseudo-religious teenagers. The pulsating hive of pubescent activity was corralled by a man on stage known as a youth pastor. The evening was filled with all kinds of activities: a band playing loud music, silly games that I was much too cool for then (but greatly enjoy in my late thirties), a finger-wagging sermon, and a van ride home. If you know, you know.

I went the first time because I was bored; I went back because the girls were loose and liked to do stuff in the back of the church van. The Jesus figure never even registered in my teenage brain. I only attended adult church once during this time and would have chewed my right arm off to escape the boredom of it all.

With the threat of prison looming overhead so many years later, I begrudgingly sat through the daily Bible studies, bi-weekly church services, and constant prayer meetings. Every prayer was eternal, every song unending, every sermon melting me into a viscous puddle of boredom in the pew. To this day, I can't comprehend why non-Christians go to church.

One night, after yet another mandatory and uneventful church service, a verbal altercation with another resident turned physical, per the usual. I was a tough hang, apparently, very prone to offense and violent outbursts. I was going to be kicked out of the program and sent to the penitentiary. I was terrified. I fled…

I'm walking down the middle of the road, in the middle of the night, in the middle of nowhere Alabama, covered in blood; I collapse as I begin to convulse violently on the pavement. I cry for a long time. I am finally and fully broken. And angry. And lost. And hopeless. I cry and cry and cry, heaving the sorrow of my sad soul out into the cold night air. All the sin, suffering and brokenness of my life finally overwhelm me. In a moment of absolute desperation, I cry out to God. I tell God that if He is there—if He is really real—then He has to do something, because I can't keep going. It's too hard. Help me.

I am, once again—like so many years ago on that cold bathroom floor on Albemarle street—laying on the ground praying for God to save me.

I wish I could tell you that the sky cracked down the middle as the voice of God thundered out to me with pristine clarity. I wish I could tell you that I heard a still small voice speak to me in the deep dark night. I wish I could tell you that anything—anything at all—happened to me in that moment of desperation. But nothing did. Melodrama rolled listlessly into anti-climax. I didn't move for a long time. I lay there, sniveling, so depressed that I didn't care whether I lived or died.

Finally, I pick myself up off the pavement, walk slowly back to the facility, and beg for permission to come inside and bed down for the night. I go to sleep not caring at all if the sun will rise in the morning. Life, death, it's all the same to me. All of life is suffering. All I feel is pain. At some point in the early dawn hours, I fall asleep.

And then I wake up.

Awake, O sleeper,
and arise from the dead,
and Christ will shine on you.

Eph. 5:14

Have you ever wondered what it must have been like for Lazarus to get up out of the grave? Dead as a doornail, and then awake. What's it like to rise from the dead? I can tell you. When I woke up that day, I climbed out of the grave like Lazarus. The voice of Jesus thundered out across the valley of death and caused my dry bones to live. Behold, the old had gone, the new had come. My eyes were filled with light and life and joy and peace and every good thing from the Father of Lights. I went to bed with a heart full of malice, hatred and pain, but woke up with a new heart and new eyes. The only thing I knew in the whole wide world was that Jesus had saved me from my sins.

Therefore, if anyone is in Christ, he is a new creation. The old has passed away; behold, the new has come.

2 Cor. 5:17

THE GOSPEL THAT ALMOST
KILLED ME

I'm in a bathtub. I can't get up. I feel like I'm about to die. The diagnosis? Mercury poisoning. The water in the tub has grown cold. I've been marinating in my own soup stock for hours on end, unable to move or call for help, floating in and out of consciousness. Whenever I can concentrate, I pray.

Please save me Jesus. Please heal me Jesus. I repent. I put my whole heart into prayer right now, and I cast out any sin, doubt and fear. I know you can heal me. I know you will heal me. I'm believing that all of the promises of God are yes in Christ Jesus. Amen.

My mother's keys rattle in the doorknob and the door thuds shut in the distance. I hear her purse slide across the counter and her keys land next to it. I barely recognize her figure as she tries, with all of her wiry might, to pull me out of the tub. We have to go to the hospital, she insists. I refuse. Jesus is my doctor. I know that he will heal me.

I'm fresh out of jail and back in the same projects I once stomped around like a tiny teenage giant. I'm a Christian now, which means that instead of dealing drugs and robbing people at gunpoint, I preach the gospel and rap to the neighborhood kids about Jesus; pants sagging, hat backwards, shirt off, gold teeth (with vampire fangs, thank you very much), and an orange Gideon Bible in my hand. I walk around most days hoping and praying for the opportunity to share Jesus with someone new.

I don't know the Bible. I've never heard the story of salvation. Creation, fall, redemption, restoration. Never heard of 'em. Father Abraham is foreign to me. The names of the twelve disciples are a mystery. I know there's a Matthew in there somewhere. I've heard of Noah's Ark and I know that Jesus is God. He died on the cross to save the world. So there's that. I sit in a small Bible study wherein a young gentleman explains to the group that Jesus was a Jew. I raise my hand and, without waiting to be called on, inform the Bible study leader that he's wrong. Jesus was not a Jew; he was a Christian. It's right there in the name: "Christ…ian". Mental note: Don't listen to this idiot.

I visited several churches soon after salvation; the experience was uniformly bad. A scrunched-up nose here, a side-eyed glance there, and a great many soccer moms clutching small children and purses tight to their bosom. I get it. I looked like a drug dealer. I was a drug dealer. One day I was walking around with a gun on my waist, the next day I walk into church looking for a new family. We were both scared and unsure of what to do next.

It was during this time I met Roger. Roger was the first professing Christian to show me kindness. He invited me into his home, bought me lunch (Taco Bell, if you must know), and talked to me about the Bible. Roger was the real deal. Or so I thought…

Roger indoctrinated me with the prosperity gospel. He taught me that Jesus wanted me to be happy, healthy and wealthy—that Jesus died on the cross so that I could live the blessed life of material prosperity. I was all in. Who wouldn't be? You're telling me that Jesus wants me to be rich? Tell me more!

> They will follow their own desires and will look for teachers who will tell them whatever their itching ears want to hear.
>
> 2 Tim. 4:3

I didn't grow up in the church. I grew up with an atheist Catholic grandmother and a nominal Catholic mother. I never went to church or vacation Bible School. Reading the Bible was like reading a German refrigerator manual. Upside down.

I was the posterchild of the prosperity gospel. I read all the source material from authors and books you've probably never heard of, but I also followed the fan favorites: Joel Osteen, Joyce Meyer, etc. When I was sick, I searched my heart for hidden sin. When I was broke, I rebuked Satan and his poverty schemes in the name of Jesus. When I didn't have the victory, I claimed the victory by the blood of Christ and the power of His cross. Yes and amen.

And yet, it wasn't working. I couldn't make sense of my sickness, my poverty, my lack of health, wealth, and victory. I was, to my knowledge, doing everything right, following the recipe to a T. As is the case in the occult, whenever I would ask questions I was told that the problem had to be with me because the system was tried and true. I needed to search my heart for sin and doubt and stop questioning the theology.

THE SECOND-BEST THING

I married my wife, Amber, at the age of nineteen. The second-best thing that ever happened to me. (The first being Jesus; duh.) We dated briefly in high school, but I cheated on her and we broke up. Before the breakup I would write her terrible love poems about the color of her eyes (your eyes are as brown as...that kind of thing), and she even planned our wedding in fifth period home economics. We still have the scrapbook in the attic. We look at it every few years and laugh. But like I said, we broke up in high school, and it wasn't pretty. She hated me, I hated her, and all of the ordinary high school drama ensued...until the day I got kicked out of school for selling drugs. But I digress...

We reunited in the parking lot of a Cracker Barrel a few years later. She saw my butt from a distance and thought it was cute. Her eyesight was perfect. Here's the story of how I fell in love with her.

Amber invited me to her college ministry, which I thought was odd, because she wasn't a Christian. I went and shared my testimony with the group of college-age Baptists, and noticed that she and her boyfriend were very physically affectionate. Too physically affectionate. Within a month it was revealed that they were living in sin. Soon after, Amber showed up at Cracker Barrel, where I waited on her, shared the gospel with her, and gave her my phone number. I told her to call me if she ever needed anything.

The first night she called I didn't recognize her voice. She asked if I wanted to hang. I did, but she would have to come pick me up because I didn't own a car. We talked deep into the night that night, and for many nights after. Amber had feelings for me, but I was determined to be single for life. Me and Jesus all the way. I told her this over and over again, to the point of being obnoxious.

Late one night we find ourselves in my apartment. I realize that somewhere along the way, Amber has gone from being a nominal Christian to a born-again Christian. The gospel has become real to her, which has caused her beauty to become real to me. I sit looking at her, and in a moment, am thunderstruck by the hidden, imperishable beauty of her soul.

I tell her that I am going to marry her. And I do. We are married within the week, eloping at the Hartselle wedding chapel, the finest and fastest way to get married in North Alabama. It was all so beautiful and trashy and stupid in equal measure. But God was with us. We are still madly and deeply in love in the only way you can be in your late thirties. My butt is still cute, she is still ravishing in her godly glory, and the grace of God looms large in our marriage.

> Let your adorning be the hidden person of the heart with the imperishable beauty of a gentle and quiet spirit, which in God's sight is very precious.
>
> 1 Pet. 3:4

THERE BUT FOR THE GRACE
OF GOD GO I

I've messed up a lot as a husband. I've dropped the ball in some pretty big ways. I've indulged in pornography. I've been addicted to the internet. I've been impatient and unkind. I've...well, let's just say that I've pretty consistently failed to love my bride with the sacrificial love of Christ. But perhaps the biggest mistake of all was teaching her a false gospel.

I discipled Amber in the prosperity gospel, and she followed me in humble love and submission. But one night, I crumbled at her feet, tearfully confessing the terrible truth that I had failed her as a husband. She anxiously inquired what I could possibly mean. I told her that my main responsibility as a husband was to wash her with the water of the Word, to teach her and lead her in the one true gospel of Christ. But I had failed her, and I wanted, no...I needed her to trust me to try again. Could she?

THE EVERGREEN STATE

Seattle is terrible. (Sorry, I can never pass up an opportunity to say something bad about Seattle.) Amber and I are stationed in the Seattle area with the Army, and because Washington state is so cold, wet and grey, we spend most of our time indoors. We have no friends or family here, so I spend way too much time on the internet. One evening, as I peruse the barren hinterlands of Myspace, I come across a video of a tiny old man absolutely decimating the prosperity gospel. Here's a sampling:

> I don't know what you feel about the prosperity
> gospel—the health, wealth and prosperity gospel—
> but I'll tell you what I feel about it: hatred. "Believe
> this message, and your pigs won't die and your wife
> won't have miscarriages, and you'll have rings on
> your fingers and coats on your back." That's coming
> out of America—the people that ought to be giving
> our money and our time and our lives, instead selling
> them a bunch of crap called "gospel."

The man is John Piper, and the video was the beginning of the end for me and the prosperity gospel.

"Hey, babe. We need to talk. I think I've been teaching

you a false gospel. Can you ever trust me to try again?"
By God's grace, she says yes, and I've been trying to love
her with the truth of the gospel ever since, and (once again)
by God's grace, getting it more right with each passing day.

> Husbands, love your wives, as Christ loved the church
> and gave himself up for her, that he might sanctify her,
> having cleansed her by the washing of water with the
> word, so that he might present the church to himself
> in splendor, without spot or wrinkle or any such thing,
> that she might be holy and without blemish. In the
> same way husbands should love their wives as their
> own bodies. He who loves his wife loves himself. For
> no one ever hated his own flesh, but nourishes and
> cherishes it, just as Christ does the church, because
> we are members of his body.
>
> Eph 5:25-30

THE ARMY

"I, Sean DeMars, do solemnly swear that I will support and defend the Constitution of the United States against all enemies, foreign and domestic; that I will bear true faith and allegiance to the same; and that I will obey the orders of the President of the United States and the orders of the officers appointed over me, according to regulations and the Uniform Code of Military Justice. So help me God."

In January of 2007, I join the Army. So does my wife. We make the decision on a whim in the drive-thru line of our local Chick-fil-A. The one by the mall. Not smart. (The Army thing, not the Chick-fil-A thing.) We can't afford Chick-fil-A, but we have a gift card. We've just donated blood because we were promised a free chicken sandwich. A strange thing, really, to trade a pint of one's own blood for a chicken sandwich. But it was God's chicken, and it was totally worth a pint a piece. But back to the Army...

I am nineteen with no career prospects, no education, no opportunities, and less than no money. We live in a roach-infested apartment, drive a car with brakes that never work when you need them to, and we have no hope of anything better on the horizon. Jesus had saved me from my sin, but I have a long way to go before I figure out how to make a living without selling drugs.

I work at Cracker Barrel for a few months. They fire me. (As they should have.) I eat scraps off plates, show up late to work, and have some...um...let's just call them "eccentricities", remnants of my street life that I'm still trying to shake off to this day.

I then work as a substitute teacher, which doesn't say much for the standards of public education in the state of Alabama, nor the discernment of those in charge of hiring for the Morgan County school system. I last three months. And so it goes. I work one dead-end job after another: From Subway to vacuum cleaner sales; I do it all. Until one day, when I'm offered free Chick-Fil-A at a blood donation center outside of Wal-Mart. (The new one, on 6th Avenue.)

We spent five years in the Army. I was a combat medic, which meant that Iraq was a lot of fun, but stateside service was boring in the extreme. I was a good medic, but a bad soldier. It was during our deployment that the Lord began to incline my heart towards missions.

THE GREAT COMMISSION

Allahu Akbar - God is Great

Ashhadu an la ilaha illa Allah - I bear witness that there is no god except the One God.

Ashadu anna Muhammadan Rasool Allah - I bear witness that Muhammad is the messenger of God

Hayya 'ala-s-Salah - Hurry to the prayer (Rise up for prayer)

Hayya 'ala-l-Falah - Hurry to success (Rise up for Salvation)

Assalatu khairum-minan-naum - Prayer is better than sleep (This part is only recited for morning prayers.)

Allahu Akbar - God is Great

La ilaha illa Allah - There is no god except the One God

These are the words of the *adhan*, the Muslim call to prayer. I hear them five times a day, every day, during our ten-month deployment in Mosul, Iraq. Five times a day I hear the toll of eternity's bell. Five times a day I am reminded that nearly two billion Muslims in the world reject Jesus as the way, the truth and the life.

BOMBS AWAY!

I'm sitting at the computer working on closing out a patient's file when the entire building begins to shake. The doors fall from the emergency room entrance, kaleidoscoping the glass into the triage bay. Without waiting for instruction, the medics, nurses and doctors begin to prep the patient bays. Casualties are incoming. Fast. Either a mortar has landed right on top of us or a dump truck bomb has blown up in the distance. Either way, we need to get ready. Blood bags, check. Crash cart, check. OR prep, check.

I still have my combat boots from that deployment, and those boots are still stained with the blood from the patients we treated that day. And many days after. Death is a part of war, and I saw enough of it to last me a lifetime.

Seeing death does something to you. It moves you past the tip of your nose, compelling you to consider that which you constantly push into the forgetful recesses of the heart and mind. Death brings eternity to bear on your conscience like nothing else can. I can't stop thinking about the depth of eternity, the immediacy of the Great Commission, the dark reality of hell, the glorious power of the gospel to save, and the billions of unreached souls who need to hear it.

Deployment ruined my life plans. Prior to Iraq, the plan was simple: twenty years in the Army, retire at 39, enter another field, work another twenty years, and retire twice by the age of 59. I had it all mapped out. Live comfortably off two retirements, travel the world, eat good food, and live the American dream until death. That was the plan. But then the reality of death burrowed itself down into my soul. I knew that if my life was going to count, it had to be about more than the American dream.

The calls to prayer were fascinating at first. And then annoying. And then haunting. Five times a day. Every day. I didn't know what the muezzin were saying, but I knew what Jesus had once said to His disciples. The harvest is plentiful, but the laborers are few. And so we began to pray, asking the Lord to lead us into the heart of spiritual battle. I knew that my time as a soldier was done. I had to give my life to something more, something eternal.

...therefore pray earnestly to the Lord of the harvest to send out laborers into his harvest.

Matt. 9:38

HER DEATH

March 13, 2010. I sit on the bed next to my mother as she lies dying of cancer. She weighs eighty-five pounds (at most) and is pumped full of every medication under the sun. Her eyes are open, but unseeing. Her mouth is dry. Her lips are cracked. Her breathing is rapid and shallow. Doctors call this kind of breathing "agonal respirations", the natural and final reflex of a dying brain. I sit with her for some time, administering morphine under her tongue, wetting her lips, holding her hand, kissing her forehead... until finally the breathing stops.

I weep.

My ladybugs will never know their grandma.
They will have many grandmothers in
the Lord, and for that I am thankful. The
generational sins of my family have, by God's
grace, stopped with me. The cycle is broken.
The curse has been lifted. And now I pray,
"Lord, bless them and keep them. Make your
face to shine upon them. Be gracious to them.
Give them peace. Amen."

A TALE OF TWO SEANS

We've covered a lot of ground so far, and I pray that you've tasted the grace of God to the superlative degree. But I hope you're still hungry because the feast has only just begun. Consider more of God's grace in the tale of two Seans.

Both Seans lived in the same neighborhood, just two doors down from each other.

Both Seans lived under the same economic hardships. (Section 8 housing, food stamps, free lunch, etc.)

Both Seans received the same level of education, dropping out of school as soon as the law would allow.

Both Seans come from fatherless homes.

Both Seans grew up with drug addicted mothers.

Both Seans were angry and loved to fight.

Both Seans used drugs to escape the pain, and sold drugs to support their addiction.

Both Seans committed violent crimes, and would lie, cheat and steal to get whatever they wanted.

This is the story of me and my childhood friend, also named Sean.

One Sean is the author of this book. Happily married with two beautiful children. A pastor. An author.

A mediocre photographer and slightly–above–average jiu jitsu athlete. Most importantly, a recipient of God's loving grace in Christ.

The other Sean is in prison, where he will spend the rest of his life for murder. My prayer is that he repents and that, even if he spends the rest of his life in prison, he will spend the rest of eternity with the Lord.

Why?

Why am I here and he there?

This is, in one sense, the nagging question of all of salvation history, is it not? Why do the disciples believe, but the pharisees don't? Why did Abraham listen to the voice of the Lord, but not Lot? Why did Esau choose soup, but Jacob choose blessing? Why did the word of the Lord soften the heart of Moses, but harden the heart of Pharaoh? Why did Judas walk out into the night (John 13:30), while Peter remained in the light?

On the last day, we will stand before the judgment seat of Christ where the sheep will be separated from the goats. Some will burn like chaff; others will be gathered into glory. On that day, and for many days after, we will still be asking the same question.

Why me?

> …he chose us in him before the foundation of the world, that we should be holy and blameless before him.
>
> Eph. 1:4

Why me?

> …even when we were dead in our trespasses, [he] made us alive together with Christ.
>
> Eph. 2:5

Why me?

In love he predestined us...

Eph. 1:5

Why Abraham and not Lot?
Why Jacob and not Esau?
Why Moses and not Pharaoh?
Why Israel and not the nations?
Why the disciples and not the pharisees?
Why you?
Why me?
Because God. That's why.

> "Having been predestined [for salvation] according to the purpose of him who works all things according to the counsel of his will"
>
> Eph. 1:11

You may not like it, you may struggle to understand it, you might deny it, but the one thing you cannot do is change it. The perfect and eternal will of God has determined, in love, from eternities past, to save all who have been given to Christ.

> In love he predestined us for adoption to himself as sons through Jesus Christ, according to the purpose of his will, to the praise of his glorious grace, with which he has blessed us in the Beloved.
>
> Eph. 1:4-6

This theology goes by many names, but the best name is the biblical one: Grace. Will you receive it? The offer is free. Kind of. You do have to die. Die to sin and self and everything in you that is not of God. But even your ability to go into the grave is a gift freely given. So, will you do it? Will you give up this mortal life and gain eternity with God?

Your life is like a mist, friend; here today and gone tomorrow. Whether you choose Christ or reject his love, you will soon die. Just like everyone else. You'll be gone before you know it.

We experience death a thousand times before we die, do we not?

Every good meal comes to a last bite.

Every fun and restful vacation has a last day.

Every great movie must eventually roll the credits.

Every easy season of life is soon met with a time of trial.

Every amazing show has its final episode.

Friendships fade.

Body parts fail.

Memories evaporate into thin air.

When we experience these little deaths in our lives, most of us are not consumed with grief. There will be another movie, another show, another vacation, another friend, another bowl of ice cream. The sadness we feel is a brief tinge of grief, a small glimmer of anxiety. But the final death, the death that all of these little deaths point to, that death terrifies us.

Why?

Because it's permanent. It is irreversible. There's no going back. There's no trying again. There's no do over. Death is so scary because it cannot be undone.

Even if you get everything you want out of life, everything you believe you need to be fully happy, in the end it will never be yours. The more you have, the more you have to lose. The more you love what you have, the more deeply it will hurt when you lose it. And you will lose it. All of it. All the knowledge you've amassed, all of the wealth you've accumulated, all of the skill you've accrued, all of the relationships you have built, all of the possessions you have acquired...all of it. Gone. Irreversibly, irretrievably gone. At the end of the day, our impending death, if we're willing to be honest with ourselves, should rob us of any and all joy in this life.

Unless...

Unless there is life beyond death. Unless there is a resurrection. Unless there is a life beyond this life, beyond this world, beyond this flesh. Hear this promise of life after the grave from Jesus, the one who put death to death and overcame the grave by passing through it and coming out the other side victorious.

> I am the resurrection and the life. Whoever believes in me, though he die, yet shall he live, and everyone who lives and believes in me shall never die. Do you believe this?
>
> John 11:25-26

GIRD UP YOUR LOINS

I know, beyond a shadow of a doubt, that a demon is in the room with me. I can't speak. I'm unable to move. I can barely breathe. My heart cries out for the Lord Jesus to be my shield, and He is. The experience is over within moments, but the impact remains with me to this day. It's our first night in the country. We're staying in the mission house in Lima, Peru, making our preparations for the jungle. We go to bed early, exhausted from travel. I wake up in the presence of evil, but go back to sleep in complete peace.

I now know what God was doing for me that night; He was reminding me, waking me up to the reality of spiritual warfare that somewhere along the way I had forgotten. I had somehow come to believe the lie that everything would be fine as long as all of my theological ducks are in a row.

Wrong.

Spiritual warfare is real, and demons aren't afraid of the five points of Calvinism. I needed to know this, really know it, deep in my bones, before going into the jungle. So, the Lord lovingly pulled back the curtain on the realm of darkness to wake me up from my spiritual slumber and prepare me for what was next.

VIVA EL PERU!

We decided on Peru for very non-spiritual reasons. We felt no particular burden for a specific region or people group, and I knew that I wasn't particularly talented in any area that might incline us to go *here* and not *there*, so the driving factors for where we wanted to go were twofold:

We wanted to go to the most unreached.

We wanted to go somewhere hard.

We didn't want to go to the hard places because we were Seal Team Six missionaries; quite the opposite. We figured that perhaps our hard upbringings and time in the military had uniquely prepared us for "the suck" (poverty, illness, lack of utilities, that sort of thing) and little else.

I smack the back of my arm to kill what I assume is my first mosquito bite in *la selva*. Within seconds, a silver dollar sized welp swells into formation on my triceps. The jungle is full of things that want to bite you. The *sancuros* (mosquitos) are the most dangerous: Malaria, Dengue Fever, Yellow Fever. The *mosquitos* (little biting flies) are the most annoying. They won't kill you, but they'll make you wish you were dead. You've heard the phrase "death by a thousand cuts"? Well, with these little guys it's "death by 1,897,473,382 bites". All day, every day.

Then, there are the ants. The army ants are the most damaging. They swarm a village like a crimson tide, consuming everything in their path. There are also the twenty-four hour ants. They bite you, and it hurts for a day. Of course, we can't forget about the snakes. Our first day in the village, I see two men each with one leg. I inquire into the missing limbs and am told of the local viper situation. Do be careful: it's a long way back to a hospital. And the list goes on: jaguars, spiders and bats, oh my! But the scariest thing about our life in the jungle has nothing to do with nature, red in tooth and claw. Our greatest fear is failure.

WELCOME TO THE JUNGLE

I wake up not knowing where I am, my pillow soaked through with sweat. It's the middle of the night. I feel something tickle my neck. Then my shoulder. Then it flitters across my face. I fly from under the mosquito net. I shake out the bedding in the dim light of my Petzl headlamp. And then I see it: a cockroach the size of my hand. Amber asks what's wrong. I tell her nothing, go back to sleep. I shake out the sheet vigorously, check under the pillow, tuck in the mosquito net, and try to go back to sleep. Operative word being try. Welcome to the jungle.

The next day, our six-month-old daughter, Patience, begins to show signs of fever. By evening, she has a 104 degree fever. We are a three-day boat ride from a doctor, and the nearest medical facilities do not inspire confidence. We don't know what to do, so we pray.

THE VILLAGE

We spend our first six months in the country learning language in Arequipa, Peru; a beautiful city, surrounded by three volcanos. I climb one of them, securing the bragging rights of doing so forever and ever. Amen. Transitioning from the city back to the jungle is a challenge, but we are brave to the point of naïveté. We arrive; we adapt. We kill the chickens, machete the fields, draw water from the well, evacuate the diarrhea, and poop out the parasites. They are the best of times; they are the worst of times. We continue to learn the language and culture, build relationships, love the people, and pray for the Spirit to move. He does, just not in the way we had hoped He would.

Six months into our time in Maypuco, the jungle village of roughly a thousand souls, I find myself in a meeting with some of the locals. We are told that if we can't get along with Jorge, we will have to leave the village. And so we leave.

KING OF THE JUNGLE

Jorge was the king of the jungle; a local Peruvian "missionary" who had been working in the jungles for over twenty years by the time of our arrival. Jorge, it turns out, was a conman, a thief, a false prophet, and a pedophile. He pumped American church money into poor jungle villages, thereby buying his way into the good graces of the locals. He came in the name of Jesus, but defamed the glory of Christ with every young woman he took advantage of.

As soon as we found out what was happening, we tried to bring his ministry to an end. It was impossible. Too many people were too heavily invested in his legacy. Too many locals were dependent on his resources. Too many pastors were too afraid of the consequences of cutting ties. And so, one weekday afternoon, we sit in a circle with several village leaders telling us that we need to get along or get packing. We pack.

And if anyone will not receive you or listen to your
words, shake off the dust from your feet when you
leave that house or town. Truly, I say to you, it will be

more bearable on the day of judgment for the land of
Sodom and Gomorrah than for that town.

Matt. 10:14-15

COMING (BACK) TO AMERICA

I thought I was going to spend the rest of my life on the mission field. But just shy of four years into our journey, we found ourselves flying home. Broken. Low. Dejected. The people group we set out to reach is still unreached. We failed.

I ask myself, "Was it worth it?" My theology says, "Yes! Yes, yes, yes! A thousand times yes!" The Scriptures tell me that:

I have to lose my life in order to find it. (Matt. 16:25)

I have to count the cost of serving Him. (Luke 14:25–33)

Success isn't always what we think it is, and seed-sewing is just as important as watering and branch-pruning. (1 Cor. 3:6–9)

Pain is temporary, and nothing compared to the glory that awaits us. (2 Cor. 4:17–18)

God's Word will not return to Him void, but always does its work. (Isa. 55:11)

I believe these truths with all my heart, but struggled to believe them in my brokenness. Sanctification, after all, is learning to grasp with our hearts what we know to be true in the Word.

FATHER HUNGER

It's a strange thing to lose a father that never was. How do I tell the story of my "not dad"? Like this, I guess...

"Hi, Sean. It's me, Caesar. I'm your dad. How are you?"

I am thirty years old when I hear my father's voice for the first time. It's Christmas Eve, and I see a number from Las Vegas pop up on my caller ID. The conversation is short and awkward. He is my father; he's been wondering about me all these years. Would I like to come see him? Within the week, my family is on a plane to Las Vegas where I will meet the man I've been told my entire life is my biological father. Here's how it happened.

After returning to the United States, our family began to rebuild our lives in Alabama. We were loved well by our local church and given everything we could possibly need to build a new life in Alabama. Upon returning, I would regularly share my testimony with various church members during fellowship. I always tell the story the same way: my mother was a drug addict; my father was a drug dealer. He knocked her up and then bailed. I was raised by a single mother; I've never met my father.

After sharing my testimony one evening over dinner, the father of the family asks me if I would like him to find my father for me. I tell him that I would very much like that, and that I have tried to do so on my own over the years, to no avail. He tells me that this kind of thing is in his wheelhouse, and that, no promises, he will see what he can do.

Two weeks later, on Christmas Eve, I get a phone call from the man I think is my father.

JERRY SPRINGER-ESQUE

I open the envelope containing the results of the DNA test. There is, according to science, a zero percent chance that Caesar is my father. The name on the birth certificate tells me that Caesar is my father, but the DNA test before my eyes tells me that he isn't. How is this possible?

In the end, Occam's razor bypassed the Gordian Knot mystery of my real father. My mother was promiscuous. She took multiple lovers, but only told one man that he was the father. Maybe she knew it was a lie. Maybe she didn't. Maybe Caesar was her best guess. Eeny meeny miny…you're the father. Caesar was just as surprised as I was, and maybe just as disappointed.

Caesar is a middle-aged Argentinian man who talks, speaks, and dresses like someone who had made a fortune and then lost it all to misfortune. He is proud to be my father, and is willing to work at a real relationship, even after all these years. He is nonplussed at my faith, but willing to abide much awkwardness for the sake of his long-lost son. The results of the DNA test crush him. I have lost my father; he has lost his only son.

I haven't spoken to Caesar in six years. He is not my father; I am not his son. Which leads me to wonder, who is my father? I'll probably never know in this life. It shouldn't still hurt this bad, but it does. Whom do I belong to? Who gave me life? Where is my dad? I wonder what he's like. Does he even know I exist? Has he tried to find me as hard as I've tried to find him? Would he love me if he knew me?

I still hunger for the love of my father. Or any father for that matter. I project this desire onto the strong male figures in my life. Will you be my dad? Will you be my dad? It's unfair of me to ask that of them, and yet, I still find myself hoping that some mighty man of God will adopt me into his love. Can you adopt a thirty-six-year-old? I never ask them directly, and they never formally reject me, but it still hurts like fire.

A EULOGY FOR THE FATHER
THAT NEVER WAS

I'm an imposter. At least that's how I feel. Not always, but often. I have no secret sins or hidden addictions, but I can't shake the feeling that I'm half the man I'm seen to be.

I'm a father. At my best, *I feel* like a good dad. Those are the best days. I scratch my elder daughter's back. I kiss my youngest on the forehead. I tickle and squeeze and tease and discipline and hug and love and watch them grow into women. My little ladybugs.

I'm a husband. I'm a pretty OK husband...except when I'm not. My wife sees me. She loves me. Grace and grace again. We make love, balance the budget, and get on each other's nerves. Butt pinching is always on the menu, date night when we can afford it. We rarely fight, but when we do, we do it right. We don't spend enough time together, and yet, we have more time than most.

We grow old, never feeling like we will get there. If we do, it will be glorious.

I'm a pastor. Shepherding God's flock is the lightest burden God's ever carried for me. And yet, I fear that one day it will all come crashing down around me. Why?

I don't know. I've always felt that way, always carried this fear.

"Who am I to lead God's people?" The answer comes clearly, "No one."

The apostle asks, "Who is sufficient for these things?" I respond, "Not me!"

The apostle responds, "Christ is your sufficiency." He better be, or I'm not going to make it.

I'm a writer. I loathe the blinking cursor, but I can't stop writing.

Type, delete.

Right click. Drag. Delete.

Cut. Scroll. Paste.

Edit. Undo typing...undo typing...undo typing.

"What's new on YouTube? Would Hemingway watch YouTube? Yeah, I bet he would."

Maybe I could write a book about *this*, or an article about *that*! But then there's the editors.

insert foreboding music.

Red lines and parenthetical comments. "Don't say it *that* way, say it like *this*."

OK. Humility. Listen. Read. Consider...disagree. DIS-AGREE!

Doubt. Second guess. Humble myself. Submit.

"Or should I?" Good writers give good editors as good as they get! "Am I a 'good' writer?"

What would Hemingway do?

I'm average. I've never been great at anything, and rarely have I been good at something. I work twice as hard to accomplish half as much. It's embarrassing. Occasionally,

I allow myself to hope that I'll rise above average in one area or another. But I never do.

Average wisdom.

Average holiness.

Average intellect.

Average pastor.

Average emotional intelligence.

Average income.

Average…

Average exists on a spectrum. Some days, I'm at the top end of average; other days, I'm uncomfortably close to the lower extremity. Which means that most days, I'm somewhere right in the middle.

Average upon average.

> …give me neither poverty nor riches,
> but give me only my daily bread.
> Otherwise, I may have too much and disown you
> and say, "Who is the Lord?"
> Or I may become poor and steal,
> and so dishonor the name of my God.
>
> Prov. 30:8-9

I'm a child of God. Before I was adopted by God, I was abandoned by a man whose name I do not know. My mom kept me, but then abused me. And didn't stop abusing me until I was old enough to make her stop. Then I abused myself. *Nearly* killed myself. *Tried* to kill myself. *Couldn't* kill myself.

Average courage.

I was an orphan. A street urchin, a prodigal who hated the father he never knew. But then God came to me. He called me by my name, gave me a new name. His name.

Yahweh saves. I ran home to Him, tears streaming down my cheeks, sorry for my sins. Before God adopted me into His family I had nothing: *no* home, *no* name, *no* family, *no* identity, *no* rights, privileges or responsibilities. No inheritance.

I was a *no*-thing.

I am a son. I spent my childhood alone in my room, eating microwave dinners in front of a Zenith TV: two knobs, tinfoil antenna, and a pair of pliers to change the channel. No family dinner. No "Pass the mashed potatoes, please." No "May I be excused from the table". No "Quit hitting your sister!" Just me, my Hot Pocket (Philly Cheesesteak if you must know), and the metal TV tray that lived at the foot of my bed.

Who will be a father to me?

And now I sit in my daddy's lap. The King loves me and has made me His very own. He bounces me on His knee and scratches me on my back and lifts me up high up in the air. It hurts a little when He grabs me by the armpits, but it's worth it. The High King of Heaven! I am His and He is mine! Grace upon grace. Love never ending. A glory to behold.

REVITALIZE

Good morning, and welcome to this gathering of 6th Avenue Church of God. I stand behind the pulpit in a meeting hall with nine other people, sitting as far away from one another as possible, as if to communicate their lack of love. It's Sunday, and I'm trusting God to bring life to this church. His church. I've been the pastor for less than a month, and ten people have already left.

Is that a spiritual gift?

The church has been slowly dying for years, and for good reason. It is doctrinally apathetic, evangelistically inept, and relationally vacuum-sealed. It is gospel anemic. Grant has been performing spiritual CPR for the last two years, and by God's grace, he's kept the church from going under. But things have begun to heat up since my arrival, and we're all beginning to sweat.

Gossip and slander assault me from every side, tossing me to and fro like a cocktail napkin in a hurricane. A member stands up and screams at me in the middle of a sermon. Another member walks out in protest during a Wednesday night Bible study. Another member screams at me in the hallway outside of my office, hurling curses at me until I threaten to call the police and have him escorted off the property. Perhaps worst of all, three ladies make it their personal ministry to carry on full-volume conversations every Sunday while I preach.

And then there's the ferns.

There are no fewer than fourteen ferns on the stage. We remove one or two per month, hoping that no one will notice. The carpet in my office is speckled with something like goat's blood. The tile in the "pairs and spares" room where we teach Sunday school is stained dark urine yellow. The walls of the meeting hall are crumbling. The walls are covered in 1970's wood paneling as far as the eye can see. The stain on the back wall is massive and moldy. We don't need an interior decorator; we need a ghostbuster. The building is in a state of complete disrepair, a living parable of how the spiritual can affect the physical, and vice versa.

But we're not done yet.

The coffers are empty. There may be a pedophile in the church. An elder proudly proclaims himself Pelagian, a most unusual and ancient heresy. He gets points for originality, if nothing else. Every day is harder than the last. I begin to wonder if I've made a mistake in thinking I could pastor this church. I feel like I'm going under. But I never do. My head remains above the water. His grace sustains me. I put on a brave face and lead us in a prayer of confession. We sing, we read Scripture, and I preach the word of God. The ordinary means of grace. I trust that if God is going to save this church, this is how He will do it. His word will do the work if I'll just stay out of the way.

> For as the rain and the snow come down from heaven
> and do not return there but water the earth,
> making it bring forth and sprout,

giving seed to the sower and bread to the eater,
so shall my word be that goes out from my mouth;
it shall not return to me empty,
but it shall accomplish that which I purpose,
and shall succeed in the thing for which I sent it.

Isa. 55:10-11

Good morning, and welcome to this gathering of 6th Avenue Community Church.

I walk into Sunday morning service with hope spilling over the banks of my heart. I see grace abounding: resurrected marriages, pastors in training, aspiring missionaries, and addictions wrestled to the ground and suffocated by the all-consuming joy of Jesus. Like a proud father, I want to walk you around the meeting hall and introduce you to each member, telling you the story of God's grace in each of their lives. Here's how Austen got saved, here's how Ms. Janice was changed by the gospel, here's how Trent overcame the devil by the word of his testimony. I want to tell you about how Grant and Alison fought to save a church no one thought was worth saving.

I want you to meet Will and Jackie, Spencer and Katie, Brittan and Susanna, and Russell and Katherine. I wish you could go out to lunch with the Millers, or the other Millers, or the Butchers, or the other Butchers, or the *other* other Butchers, and listen to their testimonies of grace. I wish you could see what I see in our church. I can't explain it. It's like another planet; you just have to breathe in the atmosphere for yourself. It is thick with joy. Serious joy. It is heavy with the weight of glory.

6th Avenue Community Church, like every other true church, is an outpost of heaven, a manifestation of the kingdom of God. It is my home. In this house I have many brothers and sisters. This home is like every other home, very imperfect. But the love of God and the grace of Christ and the power of the Spirit fill our family from floor to ceiling. My ministry here is one of weakness. I ask, along with the apostle, "Who is sufficient for these things?" Not me.

> Not that [I am] sufficient in [myself] to claim anything
> as coming from [me], but [my] *sufficiency* is from
> God.
>
> 2 Cor. 3:5

My ministry at 6th Avenue is a microcosm of my entire life. I am nothing, He is everything. I am weak; He is powerful. I am sinful; He is holy. I receive from His open hand every good and useful thing needful for life and godliness. I sin; He forgives me. I fail; His grace sustains me. There is no weakness in me that is more powerful than the working of His great might. (Eph. 1:19)

> God is able to make all grace abound to you, so that
> having all sufficiency in all things at all times, you
> may abound in every good work.
>
> 2 Cor. 9:8

Yes, and amen.

GOD'S PHILOSOPHY
OF MINISTRY

Looking back on my story, I have often wondered why God chose to let me suffer the way He did. The answer, I think, is found in God's philosophy of ministry.

A careful study of the story of salvation—from beginning to end, if you have time—reveals that God does all things with one specific aim: that He receive the maximum glory in all things. Here's how the Apostle Paul says it:

> God chose what is low and despised in the world, even things that are not, to bring to nothing things that are, *so that* no human being might boast in the presence of God.
>
> 1 Cor. 1:28-29

This is God's philosophy of ministry. He chooses the lowly, the despised, the nothings of the world so that there might be no boasting. And friend, you better believe that if it would have happened any other way, I would have boasted over God in my salvation. I would not glory in my redeemer; I would glory in myself. God knew that if I had the chance, I would gloat over Him in my redemption.

And so, He saved me in such a way as to eliminate even the remote possibility of boasting.

This is God's MO. Consider the account of Gideon and the Midianites:

> The LORD said to Gideon, "The people with you are too many for me to give the Midianites into their hand, *lest Israel boast over me,* saying, 'My own hand has saved me.'"
>
> Judg. 7:2

I am Israel. And you are, too. Left to our own devices, we will boast over the Lord, saying, "My own hand has saved me."

God was kind to me. He whittled me down to nothing before saving me. And now my testimony is firm and clear: I have not been saved by my own hand. I could never save myself. His hand of salvation reached out and snatched me from the fires of eternal wrath. I didn't understand what He was doing while He was doing it, and I hated it all in the moment. And I hated Him, too. But when He saved me, my entire life snapped into focus. I saw, with crystalline clarity, that only through the conduit of my brokenness could the glory of His grace freely flow.

> Where, then, is boasting? It is excluded.
>
> Rom. 3:27

> For by grace you have been saved through faith. And this is not your own doing; it is the gift of God, not a result of works, so that no one may boast.
>
> Eph. 2:8-9

As it is written, "Let the one who boasts, boast in the Lord."

1 Cor. 1:31

My early years are tragic. Horrific, really. But you should know that I am not merely the victim of someone else's sin. I am also a sinner, a rebel against my maker. I was not merely wounded by the sin committed against me; I was also dead because of the sin I freely chose. I followed the course of this world and the prince of the power of the air. I lived according to the passions of my sinful flesh, carrying out the desires of the body and the mind. I was in my very nature a child of wrath, like the rest of mankind.

But God, being rich in mercy, because of the great love with which He loved me, even when I was dead in my trespasses, made me alive together with Christ, and raised me up with Him, and seated me with Him in the heavenly places, in Christ Jesus, so that in the coming ages He might show the immeasurable riches of His grace in kindness toward me in Christ Jesus (paraphrase of Eph. 2:4-6).

Have you ever noticed how often the Apostle Paul turns to praise in the middle of his letters? I love it. As he meditates on the reality of the gospel his heart overflows to the point where his pen must praise the name of Jesus. Here, consider the words of one of *my* favorite hymns:

I once was lost in darkest night
Yet thought I knew the way
The sin that promised joy and life
Had led me to the grave

I had no hope that You would own

A rebel to Your will
And if You had not loved me first
I would refuse You still

Hallelujah! All I have is Christ
Hallelujah! Jesus is my life

But as I ran my hell-bound race
Indifferent to the cost
You looked upon my helpless state
And led me to the cross

And I beheld God's love displayed
You suffered in my place
You bore the wrath reserved for me
Now all I know is grace

Hallelujah! All I have is Christ
Hallelujah! Jesus is my life.[1]

This hymn tells my story. And yours. It tells the story of every sinner saved by grace. We are all victims and rebels, at enmity with the God who made us. But God, in His invincible love, sent His only begotten Son to save us, to redeem us, to reconcile us back to Himself forever.

To Him be glory forever. Amen.

Rom. 11:36

---

1   Music and words by Jordan Kauflin © 2008 Sovereign Grace Praise/BMI (adm. by Integrity Music) Sovereign Grace Music, a division of Sovereign Grace Churches. All rights reserved.

Christian Focus Publications

Our mission statement –

STAYING FAITHFUL
In dependence upon God we seek to impact the world through literature faithful to His infallible Word, the Bible. Our aim is to ensure that the Lord Jesus Christ is presented as the only hope to obtain forgiveness of sin, live a useful life and look forward to heaven with Him.

Our Books are published in four imprints:

CHRISTIAN
FOCUS

popular works including biographies, commentaries, basic doctrine and Christian living.

CHRISTIAN
HERITAGE

books representing some of the best material from the rich heritage of the church.

MENTOR

books written at a level suitable for Bible College and seminary students, pastors, and other serious readers. The imprint includes commentaries, doctrinal studies, examination of current issues and church history.

CF4•K

children's books for quality Bible teaching and for all age groups: Sunday school curriculum, puzzle and activity books; personal and family devotional titles, biographies and inspirational stories – because you are never too young to know Jesus!

Christian Focus Publications Ltd,
Geanies House, Fearn, Ross-shire,
IV20 1TW, Scotland, United Kingdom.
www.christianfocus.com